knots, tangles, fankles

ALEX REED

V.

Published in the United Kingdom in 2021
by V. Press,
10 Vernon Grove,
Droitwich,
Worcestershire,
WR9 9LQ.

ISBN: 978-1-8380488-3-9

Cover image and design © Sarah Leavesley, 2021.

Printed in the U.K. by Imprint Digital, Seychelles Farm, Upton Pyne, Exeter EX5 5HY, on recycled paper stock.

Acknowledgements

I would like to thank the Arts Council England who provided financial support through a Developing Your Creative Potential grant to assist me in undertaking background research for this book.

The Papers of R.D. Laing, held at the University of Glasgow, are an invaluable source of material relating to Laing and Esterson. I am grateful to Sam Maddra and the staff in Archives & Special Collections for facilitating access and for their assistance.

My thanks to Keren Banning, Jo Aris, Annie Harrison, Nev Clay, Liz Stanley and Andy Wood for their careful readings of earlier drafts of the poems.

I am indebted to Sarah Leavesley from V. Press for her careful editing and help in preparing the manuscript for publication.

I am particularly grateful to Linda France for her ongoing support, encouragement and wise mentorship.

Author's Note

Knots, tangles, fankles is a poetic sequence in multiple voices, written in response to R.D. Laing and Aaron Esterson's classic and still controversial text, *Sanity, Madness and the Family* (1964). In the late 1950s, Laing and Esterson began research with the families of young women who had a diagnosis of schizophrenia. Their investigation was based around this central question: "are the experiences and behaviour that psychiatrists take as symptoms and signs of schizophrenia more socially intelligible than has come to be supposed?" *Sanity, Madness and the Family* was a distillation of their findings, containing eleven case-studies that carefully documented the complex web of communications which resulted in these young women acting in a way considered 'mad'.

All characters in the poems are fictional with the exception of Aaron Esterson and R.D. Laing. Their depiction is a fictional interpretation inspired by my research into their work.

Supported using public funding by

ARTS COUNCIL ENGLAND

Character voices

narrator

hazel

mum – Gloria Dixon

dad – Tommy Dixon

dr aaron esterson

dr ronald laing

family doctor
alf mitchell, staff nurse
barbara donnelly, occupational therapist
vernon gibson, staff nurse
suzie longstaff, student nurse
dr winter, consultant psychiatrist
the senior medical committee

47 Ivy Close

Behind drawn curtains, on swirling brown carpet,
we tread carefully in measured paces,
speak in hushed voices, turning inwards,
exchange wary glances, warning gestures.

We tread carefully in measured paces,
disturbed by chatter from a neighbouring garden,
exchange wary glances, warning gestures.
Secret gives birth, calls her child Shame.

Disturbed by chatter from a neighbouring garden,
Father rises to lock the window.
Secret gave birth and called her child Shame.
Timid of light, we shrink into shadow.

Father rises to lock the window.
We speak in hushed voices, turning inwards,
timid of light, shrink into shadow,
on swirling brown carpet, behind drawn curtains.

hazel

i will tell you my name
& ask you

to call me
by this name

so my words
might touch you

& so your words
might touch me

in return
in answering recognition

the house is stirring
kettle whistling in the kitchen

dear diary, monday 1st january 1962

stuck in this cul-de-sac
for the rest of my life

       please don't leave me here

same world passing by the window
same rain teeming on the pavement

the same noses poking through net curtains
dentures gnawing tittle-tattle

no-one to love me
no-one to love

       whenever i want you all i have to do
       is dream, dream, dream

       dear diary
       who would have me?

dear diary, tuesday 9th january 1962

is that me in the mirror
these clothes i'm wearing

i look like my mother
bobbly cardy, frock past my knees.

a department in Swan's gets the latest fashions
pencil skirts, blue jeans, all the girls want them

last Friday mum finally took me
we saw a dress, just what I wanted

red and white check, billowy skirt
the assistant held it up to me

mum wasn't sure

*well, if you like it dear
but I don't think you really do*

*we'll find something better
something more – you*

The Red Book

If you've done nothing wrong you've got nothing to hide. I found it when I was tidying her room. Poking out from under the pillow. A red exercise book with her name on the cover. *THIS BOOK BELONGS TO HAZEL.* And underneath in big black letters *PRIVATE PROPERTY.* I took a minute to rest my legs and the pages just fell open.

She'd pasted in pictures from magazines. Film stars, kittens, the Eiffel Tower. Teenage fashions from the Freeman's Catalogue, a boy in blue jeans with an electric guitar. Every other page filled with writing. Lines and lines in coloured pencil. Not even neat, a little girl's hand. But some of the things in there, I can hardly say.

daddy's knee

dear little girl   my poor little girl   come

will you come   sit here   on daddy's knee

smile   won't you smile   wear your smile

for me   we'll talk together   all that

troubles you dear   such things   you say

dear   you know   your memory is poor

you're not   very well dear   that much

is clear   you're growing   so quickly dear

to be so   like your mum   the same

as mum   when she slept   for a year

her sleeping sickness   she   couldn't

wake   and was laid   in a white bed   and

never   quite recovered   my poor little

girl   dear   the same   as her mum

come   be my   good girl   dear

help us here

star

do you know what i did one night?

while my parents were sleeping

       i slipped away

to follow a star

& see where it might lead me

i crept out through the back door
closed the gate gently

       mother's cast-off cardigan
       folded on my bedside chair

the pavement sparkling
a neighbour's dog barking

       by the light of the silvery moon

i hurried past houses
streets & streets & streets of houses

towards the centre of town

       a panda car crawled behind me

my star brought me to an office block

       this lovely shiny office block

first thing in the morning
you'll start a new life here

in a smart dress & new pair of shoes

but i never did

11

In a roundabout way

It's getting worse. She's so stubborn, contradictory. Resents even the tiniest bit of coaxing. If I try to make her do anything at all, even if I go in a roundabout way, she'll always resist me. When I suggest an early night, she'll say there's something on late she wants to watch. But if there's a nice programme we're all enjoying, she takes herself off to her room.

Now, this is the latest stage. She says she wants to be independent. Can you believe it? On Saturday I told her I'd take her shopping. We'd stop for a treat at Lyons Tea Room. I may as well have saved my breath. There was some coffee bar near Woolworths she was dying to see. I've heard about those places, they've got gangs and cliques, all sorts. Foreign nationalities. I told her straight, we'll have no more of this or you can stay home.

Do you know what she said to me? *I can do what I want!* And she took herself off without another word.

dear diary, wednesday 14th february 1962

all the kids called him peculiar
the boy i sat next to at school

shy like me, useless at mixing
but gentle & kind

we stuck together in the playground
walked home the same way for protection

one sunday morning he called at my door
left a note to say how much he liked me

for the first time in my life
i couldn't wait for monday

mum was against him from the start
a look in his eyes she didn't trust

but when i packed him in
she was all for him

such a fine young man

i should never have
led him on the way i did

"I consider that the majority of adults (including myself) are or have been, more or less, in a post-hypnotic trance, induced in early infancy: we remain in this state until – when we dead awaken, as Ibsen makes one of his characters say, we shall find that we have never lived.

"Any attempt to wake up before our time is heavily punished, especially by those who love us most, for they, bless them, are asleep."

R.D. Laing, *The Politics of the Family* (Anansi Press, 1993 edition)

a nice set-up

it was on VE Day   we met at the dance   and I

walked Gloria home   and it seemed   oh she seemed

to me   I'm not saying   I was ever   I'm not saying

she was   in love with me   but we were   young

we didn't know   the ways of the world   we didn't

dislike   one another   she wasn't   bad-looking

oh I was   no bargain   no bargain at all   but she

seemed   and I thought   this could be   nice

this could be   a really nice   set-up for me   and I

might   be able to   it might be   but frankly   it's

never been   never quite   I was   a cut below   her

parents said   I worked hard   she never wanted

never needed   even so   there are certain moments

when I sense   indifference   of a certain kind   on

my wife's part   I might go further   I might admit

in certain moments   of forgetfulness   she speaks

to me   not in the way   a wife   should speak   I

thought   with time   we might blend   we might

become   near enough   the next-best thing

the electrician

dad said he's here to look at the wiring
he's been in the house for days now

all eyes for me

in the narrow hallway
as i pass

he moves aside slightly
to let me go by

our bodies brush

i feel his gaze follow
my steps on the staircase

i don't much like
the way he watches

he's too old
but still quite handsome

while i lie alone
in the dark

the things he whispers

Mist

It was VE Day. We met at the dance. It's been such a hard time, a hard time to be young. All of us looking for a little more light. A little more fun. And he seemed, maybe he wasn't, not the best-looking boy in the world, but he was eager, and he seemed to want me. And I thought maybe there's no other boy in the world who'll want me, not in the way he seemed to want me, that night at the dance. After the last slow waltz, he walked me home.

My Father would never have let him past the door. So we stopped at the gate and he kissed me. Kissed me properly, on the lips, and I was quite merry and liked how it felt, to be kissed like that. Then not long after we were wed.

Father wasn't pleased. Never hid the disappointment. On my wedding day he said to me *You've done it now, girl. That's where you'll lie.* And then I grew tired, tired all the time, could never really seem to wake. As if a grey mist had settled around me.

Sometimes this mist still seems to shroud me.

Elimination!

Any two may play together
against the third.
The rules are simple.

Turn clockwise round the table,
horizontally, vertically, never diagonally,
vying for an advantageous position.

Players are always expected to be in role.
Anyone can make an accusation
against another who disrupts the game

by missing a turn or by failure to play.
These are not matters to be taken lightly.
If wrong, the accuser must lay down their cards,

then withdraw from the table.
The last left standing wins.
Losers must not block the doorway.

dear diary, friday 20th april 1962

this house is shrinking
till it's tiny, tiny, tiny

peg-dolls propped on plastic chairs
painted smiles on wooden faces

gazing at the tiny tv
plastic food spread on the table

tiny pictures on cardboard walls
a tiny budgie in a metal cage

when the clock pretends to chime.
tiny feet climb miniature stairs

to lie down on tiny beds
dream tiny dreams in pretend heads

Funny

None of the other girls would talk to her at school. She must have seemed a bit abnormal to them. Children are quick to recognise anything like that. They tend not to talk to a child if they think that child is funny. She used all sorts of ploys to stay at home. I had to practically prise her off me. Raise my voice. Tell her if the wag man came, it'd be me who'd be in hot water. I'd get a criminal record. How would that look? Or I'd try a bit of encouragement. Tell her about Millie Simpson. Lived just down the road. She developed a phobia about school. Apparently they had to drag her over the doorstep to make her go. But Millie Simpson became one of the leading lights. A House Captain. She was a mental case and they cured her.

kitchen sink

the father's looking   staring over
mother beside him   whispering

        you go to the kitchen   while they watch you
        the whole street   hears you thinking

you go back to the settee   sit between them
little gestures   coded signals

the mother's gazing   at your red face
inserting sounds   into your mouth

the father bends   stench of breath
you look down   at your bare fingers

        he's telling you   you're...

the mantle clock   ticks loudly
mother begins   her bedtime story

        once there was   a girl   like you
        skirt too short   shirt far too tight

        wore red lipstick   liked how it looked
        & one saturday night...

the father heaves   to his full height
walks to the window   pulls the curtains

mother stands   at his instruction
you try to   reason   it's lost

        inside you

Tittle-tattle

I've got my purse out ready to pay when I hear the pair of
them behind me.

Touched in the head....
Shouldn't be loose....

Hazel's waiting by the door, where I left her. She's
chattering away to herself, tugging at her hair with both
her hands.

You have to wonder, what kind of home....

I nearly give them a good piece of my mind, but raise my
head high and walk straight out of that shop.

tiny tears

give your little girl
the thrill of being a 'make-believe' mum

take scissors from the basket
snip her hair, poke darning needles in her eyes

pull her arms from their sockets
smash her head against the door

wrap her in a crocheted shawl
bury her in a shoebox under the rosebush

forget about her for the winter
and when you take her out again

place your finger on her lips
say *hush little hazel*

and she will smile, the same
as the first time you ever saw her

Insect

She thinks we can't hear her hovering by the door. Half the evening she's lurking in the hallway, trying to hear what we're saying. She must think we talk about her, although I've always told her *there's plenty more important than you, young lady.*

Last night I decided to try and catch her. I crept over the carpet in my stocking feet, swung the door open as hard as I could. There she was on the other side, inches from me, eyes like saucers, staring out from the darkness. I barely recognised her as my own daughter – she's so altered. A different creature. When the light from the living room fell on her, she gave such a start. Lord knows what she thought I'd do to her. She scuttled back into the dark as fast as her legs would take her. Then the door of her bedroom slammed behind her.

All the while this was going on her Dad was in his usual chair fiddling with the wireless, as if he hadn't seen a thing. But when he turned his head to look at me, I swear his cheeks were wet. Have you ever heard of such a thing? A full-grown man reduced to this.

dear diary, wednesday 30th may 1962

this room is so cold
my fingers freezing

i feel their poison
stiffen my body

my white breath
clouds the air above me

        grey stain on the ceiling
            slowly spreading

no wonder

I'm no doctor   but

there is

definitely

something   wrong

the way she   she never

used to

she's not   is she

can't be

the way she   the stuff she

it's not   it's no

wonder

I mean   to say

I'm   no   expert

but   you only   have

to look   at her

anyone   can   see

voices from the landing

they're here in the room

moving closer

       leaning over

mustn't move
they mustn't see me

                        her hands   are cold

                        her feet   freezing

                        can she   hear us

                        is she

Her body is frozen, eyes wide open.

hold my breath
they won't hear me   **Even now I hear her thinking.**

If only she listened when we told her. If she'd listened when we warned her.

my eyes are misty
sinking deeply

             dream dream dream

                  this house   was alive
                  on that day   when she

She was a perfect baby.

all they wished for
a perfect daughter

as near   to perfect

as a girl   might be

never gave trouble

in any way

After all we gave her.

I'd go   so far

as to say   that she

held us   together

God preserve us.

i have tried to be
the daughter they wanted

my

sweet

little girl

she

was

this house   became

a stranger has joined them
his cold fingers

sleeping sickness

touch my wrist

Blue distance

All of this now, this isn't my Hazel. The way she hides
herself away. She's awake all night in her blue nightdress.
Alone in the dark, turning night into day in her little room.
God only knows what goes on in that head.

Dad barged into her room last night and he caught her.
Rigid as glass by the window. Distant lights flashing from
the aerodrome, her distant eyes lit in the dark of that room.
He demanded to know exactly what she was thinking. She
just turned and said, *I don't have to tell you.*

The very next day we called for the doctor.

"The question upon which we should all be meditating is that of the ultimate truth of human reality. What is it to be human, and what am I? But in our society that is called sick. Such a society cannot survive. Nemesis is upon us."

Aaron Esterson
interviewed by Andrew Rossabi (1973) *Self & Society: The Journal of the Association of Humanistic Psychology*, 1:9

dear dr esterson
Thursday 12ᵗʰ July 1962

thank you for accepting this girl for me
she has urgent need of your attention
we met today at the request of her mother
she spoke of things I could not follow

the rambling tale of a lost little girl
at times she giggled for no reason
she also wept without reason
she said that the sun was too much in her eyes

she has begun to notice all kinds of coincidence
there is a pattern behind all our intentions
the voice she speaks with is the voice of another
she fears she will be outnumbered

the parents report they don't understand her
on examination, I found her bewildering
I gave largactil without sign of improvement
in my view — schizophrenia

Exile

'and the goat will bear all their faults away with it to a desert place' Leviticus 16:22

The ceremony is a symbolic act, resonant with meanings
prophylactic, cathartic, it functions

                          to placate the idols

at the level of understanding

                          the haunted darkness

the sensibilities of the congregation

                          play of shadows

maintaining repression of the instinctual

                          they could stand it no longer

The sacrificial exile of a living creature

                          cut off the fruit thereof

vicariously relieves

                          that it wither

the burden of guilt

                          yea it shall wither

our shame before each other

                          in all the leaves of her spring

admission interview
Monday 16th July 1962

I'm dr esterson
we haven't met
I'll look after you while you are here

> *yes*
> *my eye is much better now*

pardon
there was something wrong
with your sight

> *oh*
> *my eye wouldn't open*

your eye wouldn't open
there   was   some   interference
with your vision?

> *may i wake up now*
> *my parents are dead*

I met two worried people
a man & a woman who told me
they are your father & mother

> *doctor*
> *do you love me?*

Shadow

Looking back, she was always different. A bit of a loner. Never one for going outside with others. Not that I encouraged that. Hasn't got much of a mind of her own, my Hazel. She's easily led. I've always had to look out for her. When she was little, she'd be out in the garden, playing nicely by herself and I'd be watching from the kitchen window. Always watching, just to make sure she came to no harm.

Her Dad used to say I worried too much, that I'd make myself ill, but she was such a sensitive girl. Too sensitive for this world. Now I'm not one for mumbo-jumbo, but I had this feeling all along that there was something not quite right, something amiss inside her. It wasn't anything I could really put my finger on. Call it a mother's intuition.

Of course I was devastated when the doctor said it was schizophrenia. But if you're asking me if I was surprised, speaking frankly, I'd have to say no. Not really.

It was the very thing I'd dreaded.

bouquet

on my hospital bed
ten red roses

a little white card

to our poor, poor daughter
everlasting

first meeting

the way she sits
with a sort of smile
a stiff wooden smile

she seems so subdued
little girl
with a tiny voice

eyes open wide
she looks at me
sort of smiles

all of the time
she seems to be
quite unaware

I would say
she does not feel
in any way

yet from time to time
her eyes
fill with tears

room

do you want me to talk to you
what do you want me to say?

> this isn't a good room
> this isn't a very good room at all

> i feel sick
> may I go now?

> have you seen my baby
> i thought i had a baby

i'm not able to think
this room is so strange

> there may be a baby somewhere in this room

i can't seem to talk
without my mouth moving

can you lipread?

> what have you done to my parents
> did you poison them?

perhaps i'll go now

> i didn't mean to hurt them
> i never meant to murder them

i'm all in a muddle
may i sit on your lap?

> so many voices in this room

if you speak very slowly
if you can talk clearly

> i will try to lipread

second meeting

she sways from the waist in her chair
sways to the side
then backward and forward

limbs carried by an invisible tide
reaching for something to cling to
she moves like this through the wordless hour

then, for an instant, she lifts her eyes
as if stepping from her swaying body
to place a bright flare in the space between us

I am careful to still my breathing
not to lean forward, not to startle
with eager movement

the moment gone, she returns
to her endless swaying
small and wan, lost once more

the main hall

dusty light through steel-framed windows
criss-cross shadows over parquet floor

all these tangles to be unloosened

Life in the sun

I still get a card every Christmas.

They used to say we were joined at the hip, Edie and me. We'd chatter for hours, tell each other about all the little things we'd done, laugh till the tears streamed down our faces. I can't even remember what we laughed about. It's what it's like when you're young and you don't have a care. The world seems bright, filled with light.

She married a fella from Aberdeen who'd got her in the family way. That night at the Oxford I tried to warn her, but Edie was always one for giving the glad eye. After the war, they set off for Australia. A new life in the sun.

The last I saw of her was a few weeks after I'd been sent away. She came to visit, and got quite a scare, the state I was in. She didn't stay long, but before she left she took hold of my hand and said *Listen to me, my love, whatever you do, don't stay sleeping forever.*

As the nurse unlocked the door for her she turned and waved to me through the mist.

"we are poor indeed if we are only sane."

D.W. Winnicott
cited in *Winnicott* by Adam Phillips, (Penguin, 2007 edition)

third meeting

brought this morning
by the nurse
passive, compliant

scarcely awake
she curls in the chair
as if I'm not here

twists a lock of hair
round her thumb
rests the thumb inside her mouth

her eyes dull
empty of tears
absent of light

yesterday she raged
insisted, demanded
to go home

now crushed
she's little girl lost
given up

piggy-in-the-middle

i'm much better now

        don't you agree?

nobody ever agrees with me

mum says it's clear
i'm not well yet

there's something inside
i try to keep hidden

when i tell her
nothing is wrong

she says i'm cagey
just like my dad

dad said to me *please
help me out here*

*keep the peace
agree with mum*

       you know how she is

mum told me today
if i'm so unhappy

the door's always open
i can go when i want to

      soon as i'm better

In miniature

Each night, after brushing his teeth,
pulling on his striped pyjamas,
father opens the bottom drawer
of his bedroom cabinet to gaze at her.
He lifts her out, turns her gently
in his hand, this husk of girl,
sweet and empty, light as dust.

When he's looked long enough
he tucks her back in her cotton bed,
lays her softly down, shuts the drawer,
and all through the snore-filled night
hears her ceaseless calling.

Knots Tangles Fankles Impasses Disjunctions Whirligogs Binds

After Dr A. Esterson & Dr R.D. Laing

TWT: Told What to Think
TWD: Told What to Do
TWF: Told What to Feel
TWR: Told What to Remember
BCQ: Being Critically Questioned
NAI: Not Allowed to Initiate
IOE: Invalidating Others Experience
CAI: Casting Aspersions on Independence
CAJ: Casting Aspersions on Judgement
CARe: Casting Aspersions on Reasoning

THT: Told How to Think
THD: Told How to Do It
TWS: Told What to See
NLS: Not Listened to Seriously
BPO: Being Pried Upon
EPC: Expected to Passively Comply
IDE: Invalidating Others Right to Different Experiences
CARp: Casting Aspersions on Sense of Responsibility
CAM: Casting Aspersions on Memory
CAS: Casting Aspersions on Sanity

a history (mrs dixon)

and in your own life
you've never
had a breakdown?

> No, I haven't. Never. I did have a sort of collapse. I
> was sent for a holiday. I was all right, after a few
> months. Quite all right.

would you tell me
the nature of this
collapse

> I can't really say, it was so long ago. I was twenty,
> my husband was away. I've been favoured in
> having a husband, although he wasn't always
> home, and I...you know that feeling of not really
> belonging? I felt run down, that's the point. That's
> why my parents brought the doctor.
> A long time ago.

you felt you didn't belong
so your parents
called the psychiatrist

> No, not a psychiatrist. He was sort of a Specialist.
> He told me I had sleeping sickness.
> I got over it after a rest.

these were his very words to you
sleeping sickness
this is what he told you?

> I prayed the mist would never return.

fourth meeting

how she brightens
as he enters
comes to life

her hair still wet
carefully brushed
brown eyes shining

as we talk
she moves closer
climbs up on daddy's knee

he strokes her hair
pats her gently
smiles benignly

looks at me
as if to say
you & I

we are men of the world
all grown up
we don't get upset

over childish things
be kind
to my little girl

acting the part

is it possible   doctor   is it   at all possible

she's aware   of the fact   she is acting   a

part   why I ask   there are times   it

seems   she is   pulling my leg   as if all

of this   is a kind of joke   otherwise   you

see there are   no signs of distress   she's

ever so   pleasant   always polite   but

she   no longer   shows any desire   to

be cuddled   or cared for   no longer seems

capable   of breaking down   or shedding

tears   but you will remember   doctor

you will   have seen   how here   in your

presence   she came to me   and she   sat

on my knee   while I   stroked her hair

to comfort her   the kind of thing   we'd

have done   at home   this normal thing

not done   in years

nursing report

Sunday 2nd September 1962

unsettled evening following visit from parents
patient exhibited agitation
ideas of reference & persecution
stated that nurses are conspiring with family
offered reassurance to no effect
lack of insight into her illness
dr esterson omitted to write up sedation
so we called the duty consultant:
nembutal 100mg, as required
slept well

alf mitchell, staff nurse

Identity Politics

Born Fools, Harmless Idiots,
Imbeciles, Cretins, Dunces, Deviants,
All Four Grades of Mental Defective.
Persons of Unsound Mind,
The Morally Deficient,
(often with Vicious & Criminal Tendencies),
Tramps & Paupers, The Casual Poor.
Those That Pick Up & Smoke Dog-Ends,
Epileptics, Screamers, Cot & Chair Cases,
Swallowers of Random Objects,
Habitual Drunkards, Open Masturbators.
Long-Stay Inmates, Chronics, Incurables,
Caches of Retarded Persons,
Deprived Children (Often Illegitimate
& from Poor Families).
The Associated Problem of Fecundity
in Feeble-Minded Women.

woodentop

clackety-clack   rattity-tat
fast as my clockwork legs can take me

past the room where the nurses drink tea
a voice on the telly is talking about me

this is a story about the woodentops
mummy & daddy woodentop

their woodentop girl whose name was hazel
& the biggest spotty dog you ever did see

one day daddy came home for his dinner
mummy was busy in the kitchen

little hazel was nowhere to be seen
that girl was always disappearing

mummy woodentop said to daddy woodentop
the girl's not right, we'll have her mended

let's call for the woodentop doctor
he'll saw her head open, hack out the rot

paint her fresh eyes & a pretty red mouth
fix her with glue just like new

clackety-clack   rattity-tat
down the corridor to meet the doctor

but dr esterson didn't have a saw
never did much, just sat in his room

smiled when she came through the door
then lit up his pipe & winked as he asked

did you ever wish to be real
not made of wood?

fifth meeting

she was never allowed
to do things
in her own way

never learned
how to live
in this world

the world does not seem real for her
the people in the world
do not seem real

not knowing how
to face this world
she wishes

for a world which is always
neat & tidy
where the unexpected

simply could not happen

occupational therapy

Monday 17ᵗʰ September 1962

hazel came to the department today
there was painting, dancing
she joined in very well indeed
when the last dance ended she asked
a strange smile on her face

didn't I care that the patients were dying
she'd seen me laughing as I watched –
while the dying danced, I stood laughing
I'd made them dance at their own funeral

barbara donnelly, occupational therapist

bedside locker

a lump of chewing gum hard as a stone
a rusty key found by the laundry

a dead thing that might be a scorpion
three tiny farthings

a torn picture of billy fury
a pin for killing doctors with

a page from a book about what's going to happen
a piece of my mother's jigsaw

one thing I won't tell

nursing report
Friday 12th October 1962

hazel barged in during our meeting
agitated weepy grossly unreasonable
refused to leave when we told her
demanded to speak to the hospital matron

accused staff of withholding letters
get well cards & telephone greetings
she hasn't had a single message
since the first week she was here

vernon gibson, staff nurse

her mother's shoes

hazel's mother sits
holding her hand
does not look at her directly

only an occasional flicker
a side-long glance
towards her crying daughter

the mother's attention
is momentarily captured
by a scuffling sound

hazel has taken off her shoes
and begins to untie her mother's shoes
she is exchanging shoes with her mother

the mother looks down
in smiling condescension
as if she were an observer

viewing a spectacle
she finds faintly amusing
but not particularly so

personal questions

this is the time   I like best   this last hour

before   I follow Gloria up   when I can

unfasten my belt   loosen my collar   warm

these old bones   by the fire   fetch the packet

of Full Strength   from the sideboard   light

up   with my silver Ronson   fish the Bells

from the bureau   pour myself   a decent

measure   sip it slowly   feel the heat   clear

my head   make things brighter   when I creep

upstairs   she won't stir   wouldn't let on

even if she heard   it's been   fifteen years

and counting   not that I've got   grounds to

grumble   she's a perfect wife   in other

departments   but it's been   vexing me

since   that doctor's question   I had to   ask

him   would you please   enlighten me   what

has   any of this   got to do   with my daughter

what she talks about

her body
the veins on her arms
turn of her wrist

movement of her head and neck
how her legs feel hot
a tingle runs through them

her body isn't working
she wonders why I cup my chin in my hands
why I am frowning

she is concerned about electricity
her body is an instrument
it creates interference

she is a disturbing influence
no control over what she does
no control of her vocal cords

she is just talking
it may be nonsense
for all she knows

but she has noticed
how plants can bend and be bent
while many objects

are hard, unyielding
don't grow or change
if you bump into them

you can get hurt
many people are dead
her parents have been dead for years

she herself is partially dead

wishes to be
more dead than she is

electricity –
this is what's frightening
this is the trouble

she fears her parents can hear us
they seem so unhappy
she has spoken too much

I tell her she need not worry
neither of them have the faintest idea
what we are talking about

"There seems to be no agent more effective than another person in bringing a world for oneself alive, or by a glance, a gesture, or a remark, shrivelling up the reality in which one is lodged."

Erving Goffman
cited in *The Politics of Experience & The Bird of Paradise* by R.D. Laing (Penguin, 1977 edition)

occupational therapy

Friday 16th November 1962

hazel asked if she could do some art
I made a place for her at the table
brought over paints, sheets of white paper
she worked intently for nearly an hour

I could just make out the shape of a creature
the outline was blurry, it was hard to be sure
but I think it was meant to be a bird
and the colours were beautiful, really beautiful

when I said her picture looked lovely
she thrust the tip of the thickest brush
in a pot of red paint, then covered the paper
all over, and spoilt it – she really spoilt it

all down the sides of her face and her neck
she covered herself with red

barbara donnelly, occupational therapist

catatonia

in terms of a standard psychiatric interview
she continues to show flattened affect
rigidity of posture ideas of reference paranoia

extreme sensitivity to the presence of others
withdrawal of contact from the doctor
which might be described as catatonia

but this is not how I see her at all
I would say she is a timid girl
limited in her verbal exchanges

who seems to be searching
for words that elude her
when she speaks her voice is warm

it's not hard to see that such a girl
if faced with a straight-laced doctor
would draw herself in

close her mouth tight
a very sane way of reacting
when a psychiatrist behaves by the book

nursing report
Saturday 1ˢᵗ December 1962

hazel was all by herself in the dayroom
I suggested we walk in the hospital grounds
tried to engage her in everyday chit-chat
she pulled her hood down over her face

I told her how nice her hair was
offered to style it
she might try on some make-up
a Revlon lipstick would be perfect

on the way back she never looked at me once
her mittened fingers kept clutching mine

suzie longstaff, student nurse

transference

she enters the room
glances towards him
hesitantly

Laing is slouched in my chair
his feet on my desk
those hooded eyes

he takes her in
winks
then grins

with a wave of his hand
he invites her to sit
draws his chair forward to face her

I take the third chair
a slight distance apart
looking on

he extends his hand
reaches towards her
and she gives him her hand

seeming restless
she gets up from her chair
moves towards him

I almost speak
Laing lifts a finger
to his lips

she sits down on his lap
wraps her arms
around his waist

lays her head

on his shoulder
clasps him tightly

nuzzles her cheek
against his face
runs her fingers through his hair

Laing asks something
about her daddy
did she ever feel her daddy loved her

she gazes at him, looks over to me
with wide-open eyes
the wide-open gaze of an innocent child

wriggles away
says she needs to go now
and leaves

dirty secret

i'm beginning to see what's happening here

though he will deny it
i know that it's true

                  the way he smiles
                  when i walk in the room

                  his eyes drink in
                  every inch of me

        dr esterson is my father

he is my real father
come to find me

& take me from here
to a world that's different

from anything i've known before
with friends & books, lovely things

                  his pathetic secret loony child
                  all this dirty stuff inside her

i cry when i tell him
how hard i'm trying

                  to make my dad proud
                  be a nice loving daughter

he looks at me for a long time
then he answers

        none of us can love to order

brotherly

Laing stumbles in without invitation
Glenfiddich stuffed in his overcoat pocket
sorry pal, did a wake ye

still in the suit he wore this morning
he's been working for hours on the manuscript
there's a few things he needs to talk through

whisky propelled he paces the carpet
helps himself to my cigarettes
he's written to Sartre

been asked to Paris to meet de Beauvoir
all those fucking French intellectuals
with their semiotics and signification

he's just had a note from Gregory Bateson
about his work on the double-bind
booked a flight to Palo Alto

things are tense at the Tavistock Clinic
he's skipped a few lectures
but Rycroft and Milner will cover his back

he slips off his shoes
adopts a full lotus
quotes Kierkegaard Beckett

it's a question of comin' doon
from the surface to the centre
from which all things are emanations

I rub my aching shoulder
mention in passing my own concerns
the hospital board asking questions

he tells me I have a problem with envy

pure fucking seething Kleinian envy
not the prissy bourgeois type

he brings his nose close to mine
to kiss or crash
his forehead against my skull

and in his eyes I see agony
from his briefcase he lifts a phial marked Sandoz
two clear drops in two glasses of water

stirs them with his fountain pen
you're the only one I can talk to Aaron
we must hold together as best we can

second opinion
Friday 11th January 1963

> *Re: Hazel Dixon, dob: 3rd May 1946*
> *Date of Admission: Tuesday 16th July 1962*

the patient has shown a marked deterioration
characteristic of her psychotic illness
she is thought-disordered with rambling speech
her affect is inappropriate: she giggled
& grimaced in response to my questions
refused to believe I'm a genuine doctor
demanded instead to see dr esterson
towards whom she has an unhealthy attachment

there is a family history from mother's side

prognosis in such cases is poor

dr winter, consultant psychiatrist

the space between words

at first i wasn't sure of you

                couldn't make you out at all

constantly fishing
in your pockets for matches

endlessly smoking
barely saying a word

                it seemed i was talking to myself

but for the first time
i could hear my own voice

                i might have told you anything

that last time i saw you
we sat together in silence

                pitter-patter, rain on your window

& when the hour came to an end
you finally spoke

in your tender way

                we needed this to clear the air

The Senior Medical Committee
Monday 4th February 1963

The next item for your consideration
concerns the position of Dr Esterson,
who has been with us for almost a year.

While the extension of a medical contract
is generally a formality, in exceptional cases
there can be grounds for termination.

His conduct is exemplary:
professional, punctual, diligent, studious,
if anything, over-zealous.

He is researching the families of schizophrenics
with Ronald Laing from the Tavistock Clinic;
they believe they are breaking new ground.

He spends long hours with his patients.
I simply raise this question: can it be right
to subject these souls to so much talking?

Furthermore, he barely conceals his disdain
towards the neurological basis of our practice.
I'm not sure he understands mental illness.

With some regret, I therefore propose
that we should release him from his employment.

Is there any other business?

paraldehyde

through the wire-mesh window
ear against the door

                about me about me about me

glass ashtray hurled

                across the dayroom

they swarm out of the office

                                sleeves rolled-up

pinch my arms

                frogmarch

along the dark corridor

a nurse unclips keys from his belt

a room with no window
narrow white bed

                              padded white walls

hauling me
onto the floor

                  sweaty fat fingers

                            salt in my mouth

        the one with a swallow tattoo on his wrist

tugs my nightdress
up to my waist

                the sharp of his needle
                      ripping my flesh

rancid vinegar stench fills my nostrils

they keep me locked down as the liquid burns in

we'll not hear a peep out of this one for the rest of the shift

Almost herself

When Dr Esterson left, she was put under Dr Winter. He was different again. Very formal in his manner. He had the air of authority, you could tell he was a top man in his field.

First he gave her insulin, to put her in a coma. He told us this was the correct way to treat schizophrenia. When they brought her back to the ward, she looked like the living dead. Her Dad got really upset, wanted to take her home with us there and then, but Dr Winter explained that patients often got worse before they got better.

Then he started her on the electric treatment. This worked very well at first. Brightened her right up. But he must have given her too much. She became a bit too bright, needed injections to calm her down.

Now she's in this new phase. Almost normal. The only thing is, she's got these gaps in her memory, practically blank. Apart from that, she's much happier.

Actually, I'd say she's nicer than she's been in years.

"Throughout the history of psychiatry, there have been many male liberators – Pinel, Conolly, Charcot, Freud, Laing – who claimed to free madwomen from the chains of their confinement to obtuse and misogynistic medical practice. Yet when women are spoken for but do not speak for themselves, such dramas of liberation become only the opening scenes of the next drama of confinement."

Elaine Showalter, *The Female Malady* (Pantheon Books, 1987)

the recovery suite

sand in my mouth
my eyes flicker

                              open

splayed on the stretcher

when the bolt struck my temple

                    arms jerked legs thrashed

my forehead burning

            i have fallen from heaven

                  my nightdress is soaking

                  drenched with light

a circle has gathered around me
parents, nurses, the grim-faced doctor

                  sweet esterson kneels at the foot of my bed

                  lowers his head to kiss my cold toes

i have seen the bird of paradise

"The death of Dr Aaron Esterson, at the age of 75, marks the passing of a psychiatrist who challenged the orthodox psychiatric view of the nature of schizophrenia and its treatment. Throughout his professional life he maintained his individualistic, strongly principled contribution to psychotherapy and to the prevailing social attitude to mental illness in general…"

The Scottish Herald, 14th August 1999

my dear dr esterson

do you know what they did to me after you'd gone

i'd called to your office as usual

that foul nurse all the patients hated
stood in my way with a smirk on his face

to tell me you'd left & wouldn't be back

i pictured you in some nicely furnished room
other, less crazy, girls to see

drew criss-cross lines all over my arms

weeks later i heard the rumour
how you'd been given your marching orders

did you know my father tried to find you
though he'd always thought

you had more bats in your attic than me

he knew you were the only one
who'd ever tried to reach me

for so long i'd hated you

when he rang the hospital for a forwarding address
the voice on the line refused his request

a few years back i read the book that you wrote
with your strange friend dr laing

sanity madness & the family –
eleven girls just like me

i always wondered if i might see you one day
meeting by chance on some crowded street

& if you still remembered me, i liked to imagine

you smiled when i told you

the mist finally cleared

      i made the most of every minute

soon there'll be a tap at the door

      my granddaughter bustling in, laughing

Citations / Sources

p.7, 'dear diary, monday 1st january 1962': *"whenever i want you all i have to do | is dream dream dream"* is from the song, 'All I have to do is dream', written by Boudleaux Bryant. The Everly Brothers classic version topped the UK hit parade for several weeks in 1958.

p.8, 'dear diary, tuesday 9th january 1962': the shopping episode is inspired by a scene from David Mercer's play *In Two Minds,* which was commissioned by the BBC for *The Wednesday Play* (first broadcast on 1st March 1967).

p.11, 'star': the line *"by the light of the silvery moon"* is from the popular song of the same name, written by Gus Edwards and Edward Madden and first published in 1909. It has subsequently recorded many times, notably by Little Richard whose version entered the UK singles charts in 1959.

p.14, R.D. Laing (1993 edition) *The Politics of the Family*. Ontario: Anansi Press.

p.16, 'the electrician': this draws on an incident described in R.D. Laing & A. Esterson (2017 edition) *Sanity, Madness & the Family* London: Routledge. See chapter discussing 'The Lawson Family".

p.18, 'Elimination!': this poem incorporates rules from various board games.

p.30: Aaron Esterson interviewed by Andrew Rossabi (1973) *Self & Society: The Journal of the Association of Humanistic Psychology*, 1:9.

p. 32, 'Exile': this poem uses phrases from Aaron Esterson (1970) *The Leaves of Spring: A Study in the Dialectics of Madness.* London: Tavistock.

p.33, 'admission interview': the final line is from David Mercer's play *In Two Minds*. (See the note for p.8 above for more details.)

p. 35, 'bouquet': this is inspired by a comment by Lucie Blair, one of the women discussed in *Sanity, Madness & the Family*: "he'll remember me now and then and send me a few roses, and all that sort of thing – Poor, everlastingly ill daughter."

p.41, D. Winnicott, cited in Adam Phillips (2007 edition), *Winnicott* (London: Penguin Books).

p.45, 'knots tangles fankles impasses disjunctions whirligogs binds': the title is from R.D. Laing (1970) *Knots.* Middlesex: Penguin. The text draws from the classification of family interactions developed by Laing and Esterson for their research (from notes held in the R.D. Laing Special Collection, University of Glasgow).

p.50, 'Identity Politics': all terms in this poem are taken from Kenneth Day (2000) *Prudhoe and Northgate Hospitals: A History 1914-1999.* Northumberland: Northgate & Prudhoe NHS Trust.

p.60, Erving Goffman, cited in R.D. Laing (1977 edition) *The Politics of Experience & The Bird of Paradise* (London: Penguin).

p.62, 'catatonia': ideas of reference – a mode of thinking considered to be a symptom of schizophrenia, "You start to see special meanings in ordinary, day-to-day events. It feels as though things are specially connected to you – that radio or TV programmes are about you, or that someone is telling you things in odd ways, for example, through the colours of cars passing in the street." Royal College of Psychiatrists information leaflet on Schizophrenia, www.rcpsych.ac.uk.

p.70, 'the space between words': this was the title of a 1971 BBC documentary (produced by Roger Graef) showing Esterson's therapeutic work with a family. This family agreed to be filmed for the benefit of others in a similar position.
(The documentary is currently out of distribution.)

p.75: Elaine Showalter, *The Female Malady.* (London: Pantheon Books, 1987).

p.76, 'the recovery suite': the final line is from R.D. Laing (1967) *The Politics of Experience & The Bird of Paradise.* London: Penguin – "I have seen the Bird of Paradise, she has spread herself before me, and I shall never be the same again."

p.77: text from the obituary for Aaron Esterson, *The Scottish Herald*, 14th August 1999, https://www.heraldscotland.com/news/12275235.aaron-esterson.

pp.78/79, 'my dear dr esterson': Asked what became of a young woman whose family are discussed in detail in his book *The Leaves of Spring*, Esterson commented, "...about a year later her father got in touch with me and she was back in hospital again. He thought I was the only person who had ever been able to get through to her and he asked me if I would be prepared to see her again. I said I would but he would have to get permission from the hospital. But they didn't get permission. That's the usual ending. The hospital simply closes in on them." (Interviewed by Andrew Rossabi (1973) *Self & Society: The Journal of Humanistic Psychology*, 1:9.)

In recent years Anthony Stadlen has followed up some of the families discussed by Laing and Esterson in *Sanity, Madness and the Family*. When he spoke with Claire Church, who was 91 years old, she said of her life, "I made the most of every minute." (See Hilary Mantel's Foreword to the Routledge Classics 2017 edition of *Sanity, Madness and the Family*.)

Alex Reed is a poet living in Northumberland. In 2019 he completed the MA Writing Poetry at Newcastle University and his poems have been published in various print and online publications. His previous pamphlets, *A Career in Accompaniment* and *These Nights at Home* (with accompanying images by Keren Banning), were published by V. Press and explore themes of illness, care-giving and loss. *Knots, tangles, fankles* is his first full collection, and was written with the support of a 'Developing Your Creative Potential' Grant from Arts Council England. Alex previously worked as a family therapist in NHS, voluntary sector and academic contexts.